# So Cute! Baby Animals

# Piglets

## By Julia Jaske

Piglets like to play.

Piglets like to snort.

Piglets like to eat.

Piglets like to drink.

 Piglets like to run.

Piglets like to splash.

Piglets like to explore.

Piglets like to sit.

 10

Piglets like to walk.

Piglets like to look.

 Piglets like to search.

Piglets like to sleep.

| Piglets | run | look |
|---------|---------|--------|
| play | splash | search |
| snort | explore | sleep |
| eat | sit | |
| drink | walk | |

# 48 Words

Piglets like to play.
Piglets like to snort.
Piglets like to eat.
Piglets like to drink.
Piglets like to run.
Piglets like to splash.
Piglets like to explore.
Piglets like to sit.
Piglets like to walk.
Piglets like to look.
Piglets like to search.
Piglets like to sleep.

# CHERRY BLOSSOM PRESS

Published in the United States of America by Cherry Lake Publishing Group
Ann Arbor, Michigan
www.cherrylakepublishing.com

Book Designer: Melinda Millward

Photo Credits: © Simun Ascic/Shutterstock, cover, 1; © Nattaro Ohe/Shutterstock, 2; © Irina Kozorog/Shutterstock, 3; © Chumash Maxim/Shutterstock, 4; © Simun Ascic/Shutterstock, 5; © BMJ/Shutterstock, 6; © jadimages/Shutterstock, 7; © Budimir Jevtic/Shutterstock, 8; © HQuality/Shutterstock, 9; © Rita_Kochmarjova/Shutterstock, 10; © Bernd Wolter/Shutterstock, 11; © grandbrothers/Shutterstock, 12; © Fedor Selivanov/Shutterstock, 13; © Eric Isselee/Shutterstock, 14

**Cherry Blossom Press** is an imprint of Cherry Lake Publishing Group.

Library of Congress Cataloging-In-Publication Data

Names: Jaske, Julia, author.
Title: Piglets / written by Julia Jaske.
Description: Ann Arbor, Michigan : Cherry Lake Publishing, [2022] | Series: So cute! Baby animals
Identifiers: LCCN 2022009905 | ISBN 9781668908792 (paperback) | ISBN 9781668911983 (ebook) | ISBN 9781668913574 (pdf)
Subjects: LCSH: Piglets—Juvenile literature.
Classification: LCC SF395.5 .J37 2022 | DDC 636.4/07—dc23/eng/20220325
LC record available at https://lccn.loc.gov/2022009905

Cherry Lake Publishing Group would like to acknowledge the work of the Partnership for 21st Century Learning, a Network of Battelle for Kids. Please visit http://www.battelleforkids.org/networks/p21 for more information.

Printed in the United States of America
Corporate Graphics